GW01374927

First published in Great Britain in 1996 by
Brockhampton Press,
20 Bloomsbury Street,
London WC1B 3QA.
a member of the Hodder Headline Group,

This series of little gift books was made by Frances Banfield, Andrea P.A. Belloli, Polly Boyd, Kate Brown, Stefano Carantini, Laurel Clark, Penny Clarke, Clive Collins, Jack Cooper, Melanie Cumming, Nick Diggory, John Dunne, Deborah Gill, David Goodman, Paul Gregory, Douglas Hall, Lucinda Hawksley, Maureen Hill, Dennis Hovell, Dicky Howett, Nick Hutchison, Douglas Ingram, Helen Johnson, C.M. Lee, Simon London, Irene Lyford, John Maxwell, Patrick McCreeth, Morse Modaberi, Tara Neill, Sonya Newland, Anne Newman, Grant Oliver, Ian Powling, Terry Price, Michelle Rogers, Mike Seabrook, Nigel Soper, Karen Sullivan and Nick Wells.

ISBN 1 86019 4281

A copy of the CIP data is available from the British Library upon request.

Produced for Brockhampton Press by Flame Tree Publishing,
a part of The Foundry Creative Media Company Limited,
The Long House, Antrobus Road, Chiswick W4 5HY.

Printed and bound in Italy by L.E.G.O. Spa.

THE LITTLE BOOK OF *Faeries*

Selected by Karen Sullivan

BROCKHAMPTON PRESS

Up the airy mountain,
Down the rushy glen,
We daren't go a-hunting,
For fear of little men.

William Allingham, 'The Fairies'

Behold the chariot of the Fairy Queen!
Celestial coursers paw the unyielding air;
Their filmy pennons at her word they furl,
And stop obedient to the reins of light:
These the Queen of Spells drew in,
She spread a charm around the spot,
And leaning graceful from the ethereal car,
Long did she gaze, and silently,
Upon the slumbering maid.

Percy Bysshe Shelley, *Queen Mab*

There are fairies at the bottom of our garden.

Rose Fyleman, *Fairies and Chimneys*

Grey lichens, mid thy hills of creeping thyme,
Grow like to fairy forests hung with rime;
And fairy money-pots are often found
That spring like little mushrooms out of ground,
Some shaped like cups and some in slender trim
Wine glasses like, that to the very rim
Are filled with little mystic shining seed.

John Clare, 'Fairy Things'

By which we note the fairies
Were of the old profession;
Their songs were Ave Marias,
Their dances were procession...

Richard Corbet, 'The Fairies' Farewell'

It was soft and round, and about the colour of a ripe apricot: it was covered with fur, and had curled itself up into a round ball. 'It's only one of the air fairies,' said Mopsa. 'Pretty creature!'

Jean Ingelow, *Mopsa the Fairy*

The fairie's love of mortal commerce prompted them to have their children suckled at earthly breasts.

R. H. Cromek, *The Fairy Midwife*

The crowded boats of a fairy fleet had just arrived. On the shore stood groups of fairy ladies in all colours of the rainbow, green predominating, waited upon by gentlemen all in green, but with red and yellow feathers in their caps.

George Macdonald, *The Carasoyn*

Faeries often dance in circles in the grass which are called faerie rings and this spells danger for the human passerby. The wild enchantment of the faerie music can lead him inexorably towards the ring which, like a faerie kiss or faerie food and drink, can lead to captivity for ever in the world of Faerie. If a human steps into the ring he is compelled to join the faeries in their wild prancing.

Brian Froud and Alan Lee, *Faeries*

Peaseblossom was dressed in white, with a cloak of sunset-red – the colours of the sweetest of sweet-peas. On her head was a crown of twisted tendrils, with a little gold beetle in front.

George Macdonald, *Cross Purposes*

Once upon a time, a young maiden went to drive her father's cattle to the hill. A fairy knoll lay before her in the path she took; and after she came in sight of it, she met a band of fairies, with one taller than the rest at their head. This one seized her and, with the help of the others, took her away with him to the fairy knoll.

James MacDougall, *Folk Tales and Fairy Lore*

And by the moon the reaper weary,
Piling sheaves in uplands airy,
Listening, whispers 'Tis the fairy
Lady of Shalott.'

Alfred, Lord Tennyson, 'The Lady of Shalott'

When mortals are at rest,
And snoring in their nest;
Unheard and unespyed,
The key holes we do glide;
Over tables, stools and shelves,
We trip it with our fairy elves.

Anonymous, *The Fairy Queen*

... for it is said to have constantly imitated the voice of the servant-girl's lovers, overturned the kailpot, given the cream to the cats, unravelled the knitting, or put the spinning wheel out of order.

William Henderson,
Notes on the Folklore of the Northern Countries of England and the Borders

When oak and ash and thorn grow together, it is said that one will be able to see faeries.

Traditional

And pleasant is the fairy land,
But, an eerie tale to tell,
Ay at the end of seven years
We pay a tiend to hell;
I am sae fair and fu of flesh
I'm feard it be myself.

Francis James Child, *English and Scottish Popular Ballads*

Upon a mushroome's head
Our table cloth we spread;
A grain of rye, or wheat,
Is manchet, which we eat;
Pearly drops of dew we drink
In acorn cups fill'd to the brink.

Anonymous, *The Fairy Queen*

NE CLOKE

Strew vervain or sage and tobacco on your garden as an offering to the fairies and elementals who help it grow.

Then come you fairies dance with me a round;
Melt her hard heart with your melodious sound.

Thomas Campion, 'Song for the Lute'

And the Elves also,
Whose little eyes glow,
Like the sparks of fire, befriend thee.

Robert Herrick, 'The Night-Piece to Julia'

I met a lady in the meads,
Full beautiful – a faery's child,
Her hair was long, her foot was light
And her eyes were wild.

John Keats, 'La Belle Dame Sans Merci'

The foxglove bells, with lolling tongue,
Will not reveal what peals were rung
In Faery, in Faery,
A thousand ages gone.
All the golden claspers rang;
Only from the mottled throat
Never any echoes float.
Quite forgotten, in the wood,
Pale, crowded steeples rise...

Mary Webb

There never was a merry world
since the fairies left off dancing.

John Selden, *Table Talk*

This is Mab,
this Mistress-Fairy
That doth nightly
rob the dairy.

Ben Jonson, *The Satyr*

Fairies live so much longer than we, that they can have business with a good many generations of human mortals.

George Macdonald, *Little Daylight*

Stand or sleep under an elder on Midsummer Eve to see the King of the Faeries and his retinue pass by.

And so it was that ten or twelve small fairies appeared to rescue their kin, but since fairies cannot swim, they danced helplessly on the shore while the water grew higher and higher about the rock. The fisherman's wife was smug, and she said, 'I shall leave him there, until you return my baby.'

And the fairies disappeared and returned with her baby, who had grown in his time away from his mother, and whose cheeks were roses, whose white skin held the bloom of good health. And she thanked the fairies, and returned their bodach to them.

So the fisherman's wife, flushed with her good fortune, went back to her cosy cottage, protected from the winds which blew cold and damp from the sea. She lived there with her blossoming baby, by day combing the sands for seaweed, and at night nestling warm in her bed with her son, silently thanking the little people who had made him strong.

K. E. Sullivan, *The Fairy Changeling*

The beams overhead were crowded with fairies, playing all imaginable tricks, scrambling everywhere, knocking each other over, throwing dust and soot in each other's faces, grinning from behind corners, dropping on each other's necks, and tripping up each other's heels.

George Macdonald, *The Carasoyn*

O then I see Queen Mab hath been with you.
She is the fairies' midwife, and she comes
In shape no bigger than an agate stone
On the forefinger of an alderman,
Drawn with a team of little atomie
Over men's noses as they lie asleep.

William Shakespeare, *Romeo and Juliet*

Her wagon-spokes made of long spinners' legs;
The cover, of the wings of grasshoppers;
Her traces, of the smallest spider web;
Her collars, of the moonshine's watery beams;
Her whip, of cricket's bone; the lash, of film;
Her wagoner, a small gray-coated gnat,
Not half so big as a round little worm
Pricked from the lazy finger of a maid.
Her chariot is an empty hazel-nut,
Made by the joiner squirrel or old grub,
Time out of mind the fairies' coachmakers.

William Shakespeare, *Romeo and Juliet*

And I serve the fairy queen,
To dew her orbs upon the green;
The cowslips tall her pensioners be;
In their gold coats spots you see;
There be rubies, fairy favours,
In those freckles live their savours:
I must go seek some dew-drops here
And hang a pearl in every cowslip's ear.

William Shakespeare, *A Midsummer Night's Dream*

Fairies, black, grey, green and white,
You moonshine revellers, and shades of night.

William Shakespeare, *The Merry Wives of Windsor*

Hollyhock flowers attract money, success, and material wealth of all kinds. They are favoured by the fairies who bring luck to the home.

As a world that has no well,
Darkly bright in forest dell;
As a world without the gleam
Of the downward-going stream...

George Macdonald, *The Light Princess*

Drab Habitation of Whom?
Tabernacle or Tomb –
Or Dome of Worm –
Or Porch of Gnome –
Or some Elf's Catacomb?

Emily Dickinson

The Fairy's frame was slight; yon fibrous cloud,
That catches but the palest tinge of even,
And which the straining eye can hardly seize
When melting into eastern twilight's shadow,
Were scarce so thin, so slight; but the fair star,
That gems the glittering coronet of morn,
Sheds not a light so mild, so powerful,
As that which, bursting from the Fairy's form,
Spread a purpureal halo round the scene,
Yet with an undulating motion,
Swayed to her outline gracefully.
From her celestial car
The Fairy Queen descended,
And thrice she waved her wand
Circled with wreaths of amaranth:
Her thin and misty form
Moved with the moving air,
And the clear silver tones,
As thus she spoke, were such
As are unheard by all but gifted ear.

Percy Bysshe Shelley, *Queen Mab*

'Here Gob, Shag, Latchit, Licker, Freestone,
Greywhackit, Mousetrap, Potato-pot, Blob, Blotch,
Blunker' – And ever as he called,
one dwarf after another came tumbling out of
the chimney in the corner.

George Macdonald, *The Carasoyn*

I am that merry wanderer of the night.
I jest to Oberon, and make him smile
When I a fat and bean-fed horse beguile,
Neighing in likeness of a filly foal.

William Shakespeare, *A Midsummer Night's Dream*

PUCK: Troop home to churchyards: damned spirits all,
That in cross-ways and floods have burial,
Already to their wormy beds are gone;
For fear lest day should look their shames upon,
They wilfully themselves exile from the light,
And must for aye consort with black brow'd night.
OBERON: But we are spirits of a different sort.

William Shakespeare, *A Midsummer Night's Dream*

The land of faery
Where nobody gets old and
godly and grave,
Where nobody gets old and
crafty and wise,
Where nobody gets old and
bitter of tongue.

W. B. Yeats

In Italy there is an old tale of an exquisitely beautiful fairy who appeared to a knight with the image of the crescent moon and the Holy Grail at her feet. In her hands she held a sprig of mistletoe. She told the knight that the mistletoe was the secret of her eternal youth and beauty.

Traditional

Through the house give glimmering light
By the dead and drowsy fire;
Every elf and fairy sprite
Hop as light as bird from brier.

William Shakespeare, *A Midsummer Night's Dream*

The men were of the smallest stature, but very well-proportioned in their make; they were all of a fair complexion, with luxuriant hair falling over their shoulders like that of women. They had horses and greyhounds adapted to their size.

Giraldus Cambrensis, twelfth century

If lustie Doll, maide of the Dairie,
Chance to be blew nipt by the Fairie...

Marston, *Mountebanke's Massque*

The iron tongue of midnight hath told twelve;
Lovers, to bed;' tis almost fairy time.

William Shakespeare, *A Midsummer Night's Dream*

'It's called the Enchanted Wood,' said their father. 'People don't go there if they can help it. It's funny to hear things like this nowadays, and I don't expect there is really anything very queer about the wood. But just be careful not to go too far into it, in case you get lost.' The children looked in excitement at one another. The Enchanted Wood! What a lovely name!... 'The Enchanted Wood! We knew there was something queer about it!' 'I guessed there were fairies there!' said Fanny.

Enid Blyton, *The Enchanted Wood*

Hang mistletoe over the cradle
to prevent the theft of the child by faeries.

Anonymous

And the fairies all will run,
Wildly dancing by the moon,
And will pinch him to the bone,
Till his lustful thoughts be gone.

John Fletcher, *The Faithful Shepherdess*

Every time a child says 'I don't believe in fairies,' there is a little fairy somewhere that falls down dead.

J. M. Barrie, *Peter Pan*

We must not buy their fruits;
Who knows upon what soil they fed,
Their hungry thirsty roots.

Christina Rossetti, 'Goblin Market'

Fairy land
Where all the children dine at five,
And all the playthings come alive.

Robert Louis Stevenson, *A Child's Garden of Verse*

When the first baby laughed for the first time, the laugh broke into a thousand pieces, and they all went skipping about, and that was the beginning of fairies.

J. M. Barrie, *Peter Pan*

'Nobody Loves a Fairy
When She's Forty'

Title of song by Arthur Henley

Arthur Rackham
08

A moment after the fairy's entrance the window was blown open by the breathing of the little stars, and Peter dropped in. He had carried Tinker Bell part of the way, and his hand was still messy with the fairy dust.

'Tinker Bell,' he called softly, after making sure that the children were asleep, 'Tink, where are you?' She was in a jug for the moment, and liking it extremely; she had never been in a jug before.

'Oh, do come out of that jug, and tell me, do you know where they put my shadow?'

The loveliest tinkle as of golden bells answered him. It is the fairy language...

J. M. Barrie, *Peter Pan*

The fairies break their dances
And leave the printed lawn...

A. E. Housman, *Last Poems*

Following their bathe, the boys chased one another to get dry, dressed and began to walk slowly home. Crossing a field, MacManus's friend saw a little figure dart behind a rock. He told his companion who answered that it must have been a scarecrow flapping in the wind. His curiosity unsatisfied, the boy approached the rock to investigate, and suddenly both boys found themselves confronted with a little man about four feet high wearing a shiny collarless black coat buttoned up to the chin, and a cap. He had pepper and salt whiskers and a broad friendly grin on his face, but the boys were terrified and took to their heels as if the devil himself were after them.

Dermot MacManus, *Faeries*

If thou'rt of air let grey mist fold thee,
if of earth let the swart mine hold thee,
if a Pixie sink thy ring
if a Nixie seek thy spring.

Sir Walter Scott

I met a little Elf-man, once,
Down where the lilies blow.
I asked him why he was so small,
And why he didn't grow.

He slightly frowned, and with his eye
He looked me through and through.
'I'm quite as big for me,' said he,
'As you are big for you.'

John Kendrick Bangs, 'The Little Elf'

Beside the old hall-fire – upon my nurse's knee,
Of happy fairy days, what tales were told to me!
I thought the world was once
all peopled with princesses,
And my heart would beat
to hear their loves and their distresses;
And many a quiet night, in slumber sweet and deep,
The pretty fairy people would visit me in sleep...

William Makepeace Thackeray, 'Fairy Days'

Children born of fairy stock
Never need for shirt or frock,
Never want for food or fire,
Always get their heart's desire...

Robert Graves, 'I'd Love to Be a Fairy's Child'

I do not know why I am so sad;
there is an old fairy tale that I cannot
get out of my mind.

Henrich Heine

Get up, our Anna dear, from the weary spinning-wheel;
For your father's on the hill, and your mother is asleep;
Come up above the crags,
and we'll dance a highland-reel
Around the fairy thorn on the steep.

Sir Samuel Ferguson, *The Fairy Thorn*

Her skirt was of the grass-green silk,
Her mantle of the velvet fine;
On every lock of her horse's mane
Hung fifty silver bells and nine.

'Harp and carp, Thomas,' she said,
'Harp and carp along with me;
And if ye dare to kiss my lips,
Sure of your body I will be!'

Anonymous, 'True Thomas'

It is perfectly well known that out of Fairyland nobody ever can find where the rainbow stands.

George Macdonald, *The Golden Key*

A Golden Fairy – she is decidedly fair in colouring, full of laughter and happiness, very open and fearless in expression, and is surrounded by an aura of golden radiance in which the outline of her wings can be traced. There is also a hint of mockery in her attitude and expression, as of one who is enjoying a joke against the poor mortals who are studying her.

Geoffrey Hodson, *Fairies at Work and at Play*

Come up here, O dusty feet!
Here is fairy bread to eat.
Here in my retiring room,
Children, you may dine
On the golden smell of broom
And the shade of pine;
And when you have eaten well,
Fairy stories hear and tell.

Robert Louis Stevenson, 'Fairy Bread'

Pantomime
Pictures
A Novel Surprise Book
of Living Pictures.

Deep in the forest, at the edge of the vale
Lit by the moonlight, wings glittering and frail
There are two little fairies,
and their names you enquire?
Why they're Tixie and Lixie –
they fly higher and higher
Until in a moment they land on a branch
And they lean there exhausted,
and they pant and they pant
Then they listen quite closely, in the distance they hear
The rustle of witches who are getting quite near
They look up, look around,
and then hardly dare whisper
For the littlest sound stirs a dark wicked sister
Now witches were fairies, before they grew bad
Their wings, they fell off, and in black they were clad
Now they search for good fairies
to take back to their homes
And they turn them to witches, or nasty wee gnomes
So Tixie and Lixie are as quiet as snails
On their foresty branch, in the green-leaved dale.

Kitty Browne, 'Tixie and Lixie'